Ariadne's
Story

LEVEL TWO   700 HEADWORDS

OXFORD
UNIVERSITY PRESS

Great Clarendon Street, Oxford OX2 6DP

Oxford University Press is a department of the University of Oxford.
It furthers the University's objective of excellence in research, scholarship,
and education by publishing worldwide in

Oxford New York

Auckland Cape Town Dar es Salaam Hong Kong Karachi
Kuala Lumpur Madrid Melbourne Mexico City Nairobi
New Delhi Shanghai Taipei Toronto

With offices in

Argentina Austria Brazil Chile Czech Republic France Greece
Guatemala Hungary Italy Japan Poland Portugal Singapore
South Korea Switzerland Thailand Turkey Ukraine Vietnam

OXFORD and OXFORD ENGLISH are registered trade marks of
Oxford University Press in the UK and in certain other countries

This edition © Oxford University Press 2010

The moral rights of the author have been asserted

Database right Oxford University Press (maker)

First published in Dominoes 2007

2014 2013 2012 2011 2010

10 9 8 7 6 5 4 3 2 1

ISBN: 978 0 19 424888 4 BOOK
ISBN: 978 0 19 424840 2 BOOK AND MULTIROM PACK
MULTIROM NOT AVAILABLE SEPARATELY

No unauthorized photocopying

ACKNOWLEDGEMENTS

Illustrations by: Levi Pinfold

The publisher would like to thank the following for permission to reproduce photographs: Alamy
Images pp13 (Toreador fresco, Palace of Knossos, Crete/Visual Arts Library (London)), 32
(Ladies in Blue fresco, Palace of Knosso, Crete/Bob Turner), 53 (The Parthenon, Athens,
Greece/David Levenson); Getty Images p26 (Rhyton in the shape of a bull's head, from
Knossos, Minoan, 1700-1400 BC (marble and gold) Archaeological Museum of Heraklion,
Crete, Greece/the Bridgeman Art Library).

DOMINOES

Series Editors: Bill Bowler and Sue Parminter

Ariadne's Story

Joyce Hannam

Illustrated by Levi Pinfold

Joyce Hannam has taught English in several European countries including Greece, Spain, Turkey and the Czech Republic. She now lives in York, in the north of England, and works for the University of York providing language support for all nationalities. She has written a number of other stories for students of English, including *The Curse of the Mummy* and the retelling of *The Teacher's Secret and Other Folk Tales*, in the Dominoes series, and *The Death of Karen Silkwood* in the Oxford Bookworms Library.

OXFORD
UNIVERSITY PRESS

ACTIVITIES

BEFORE READING

1 These are some of the characters from *Ariadne's Story*. Match the names and pictures with the sentences.

| **a** ARIADNE | **b** PHEDRA | **c** MINOS | **d** DEDALUS | **e** ENARUS | **f** THESEUS |

1 [f] is a prince from Athens.
2 [ ] is a beautiful princess from the island of Crete.
3 [ ] is a clever, funny young man.
4 [ ] is a princess and the younger sister of Ariadne.
5 [ ] is a kind old man and a good teacher.
6 [ ] is the strong king of Crete and Ariadne's and Phedra's father.

2 What happens in the story? Match the two parts of the sentences.

a Ariadne falls in love with . . .
b Phedra finds out about . . .
c Minos is angry with . . .
d Enarus suddenly has to leave . . .
e Dedalus helps . . .
f Theseus comes to Crete and fights . . .

1 a terrible monster.
2 the island of Crete.
3 her friend, Enarus.
4 her sister's secret.
5 his daughter.
6 Ariadne to escape.

Chapter 1 ✛ Secret friends

When he went home to Athens, the great **prince** Theseus took me with him at first, but he later left me on the island of Naxos. Why did he leave me there? Everyone says that he was tired of me. But when we met, I was a **princess** of Crete and the most beautiful woman in the world. Was he really tired of me? Some people say that I killed myself when he left and went to Athens with my younger sister Phedra. She was only a child at the time, but it was useful to me that people thought I was so angry or sad that I ended my life then. I am old now, forty years old, and I want to tell everyone what really happened before it is too late.

My story begins long before Theseus came to Crete. When I was a child, I lived in the **Palace** of Knossos with my father, **King** Minos. He was not only the king of Crete. He was also the strongest king in the world. The other kings were afraid of him. To keep him happy, Aegeus – the king of Athens – and the kings of all the other cities had to send presents to him every year. One of the presents Aegeus had to send was seven young men and seven young women from Athens. They had to come to Crete every year and fight the **bulls.** All our people loved watching bullfights. When the boys and girls died in the bullfights, we gave their dead bodies to the Minotaur, the **monster** who lived in the **Labyrinth**, and he ate them. I usually watched the bullfights with my father, but I never thought much about those young people from far away. They came every year and they died every year, just like the flowers in the palace gardens. The **priests** told us that we must give the Minotaur young people's bodies to eat, so we gave him the dead bullfighters. People were afraid that one day the Minotaur would come out to kill people for food. So, if no bullfighters died in the bullfights for a long

prince the son of a king

princess the daughter of a king

palace a big house where a king lives

king the most important man in a country

bull a male animal like a cow

monster a large, horrible animal

labyrinth a place with lots of paths between walls where you can easily lose yourself

priest a man who works in a temple

time, we sometimes sent one of them into the Labyrinth when he or she was still alive. Of course, we didn't want to send Cretan children to the monster.

The Labyrinth was under the ground at the bottom of our palace. Sometimes we could hear the Minotaur inside it: he **roared** like an angry bull under our feet. It was a terrible noise. Sometimes little boys ran inside the great door of the Labyrinth to show their friends how **brave** they were. Those who went in far enough never came out again because they always lost their way inside. One of my father's oldest friends, Dedalus, once told me that the Minotaur had the head of a bull but the body of a man.

'How do you know?' I asked him.

'Because I was there when the monster was born, and I built the Labyrinth to be his prison and his home,' answered Dedalus. 'Your father and I put the Minotaur there many years ago.'

'But why?' I asked. 'Why not kill him if he's so dangerous?'

'This is a question that you must ask your mother,' answered Dedalus. 'But don't worry, princess. The Minotaur can never escape from the Labyrinth. Only I know the way in and out – and your father, of course. It is good that most people are afraid of the Minotaur, but you must never be. The daughter of Minos should never be afraid.'

roar to make a loud noise like a big animal

brave not afraid of doing dangerous things

2

I never asked my mother about the monster. Somehow I knew that she would not like the question.

Dedalus was a kind old man and a very good teacher. He started to teach Phedra and me when we were very young. We knew much more than most other girls, who never studied. Dedalus taught us so many things about the world outside the palace. He knew a lot about the stars and the seas and other countries far from Crete. One day, when I was about eleven, two boys joined our classes with Dedalus. One was his son, Icarus, and the other was Enarus. Enarus was the son of the High Priest at the **temple** of Dionysus, a very important man in Crete. Dionysus was one of our most important **gods** – the god of wild feelings. It was a wonderful day for me when Icarus and Enarus joined our classes. At last I had some friends, not just a boring little sister to play with. I liked both the boys, but Enarus was always special. He was clever and funny. For four years Icarus and Phedra played together, while I was always with Enarus. Dedalus didn't worry because he saw that all his students were happy, and we were still very young.

temple some people go here to pray

god an important being who never dies and who decides what happens in the world

But one day Minos was passing the palace gardens when he saw me with Enarus. We were lying and talking together under the trees at the time. Out of the corner of my eye I saw my father standing there. He watched us silently for a few moments. Then he called my name. 'Ariadne!' he said. 'Come here at once!'

I left Enarus under the trees and went to my father.

'Ariadne,' he said once I stood in front of him, 'you are now fifteen years old. When I die, you and your sister must **look after** Crete. You will need the help of strong husbands who are also princes. A prince can understand how to **rule** a **kingdom**, and his people will be your friends also.'

He looked at Enarus under the trees.

'Do you understand me?' he said.

'Yes, father,' I answered.

But of course I didn't really understand – not until the next morning when Enarus and Icarus didn't come to class. They never came again. Dedalus told me that Enarus was working with his father in the temple. I didn't see him for weeks. My life **became** suddenly boring and lonely. Phedra followed me everywhere, but I didn't want to be with her. In the end, I thought of a way to keep Phedra busy and to see Enarus again. I told Phedra that we had a new **game**. She had to take secret **messages** to Enarus.

'If anyone finds out,' I told her, 'they'll give you to the Minotaur because these are very secret messages.'

Phedra was a little afraid, but she agreed to play the game because it was so exciting. She could go anywhere in the palace because she was so small, but I couldn't easily leave the women's rooms. So she went to the temple of Dionysus and gave Enarus my messages. He gave messages to her to bring back to me. Once a week Enarus and I met in the palace gardens. I knew a quiet place very near the door of the Labyrinth where nobody liked to go. I often walked there

look after to do things for someone or something that needs help

rule to decide what happens in a country

kingdom the country of a king

become (*past* **became**, **become**) to begin to be

game something that you play; tennis and football are games

message you write this to someone

in the evenings when it was **cool.** Nobody thought it was
strange that my walks were sometimes longer than usual.

Or that's what I thought. But I forgot my little sister. One
day she followed me, and watched Enarus and me together.
She said nothing to me about it at the time, but she couldn't
keep quiet for long. With a stick she made her secret into
a picture on the ground one morning.

'Who's that?' asked a friendly **servant.**

'It's Ariadne and her secret friend, Enarus, in the garden
near the door of the Labyrinth,' Phedra said, smiling.

The servant went to speak to my father.

The next morning my father called me to his rooms.

cool not warm

servant a person
who works for
someone rich

READING CHECK

Are these sentences true or false? Tick the boxes.

		True	False
a	Princess Ariadne is the daughter of King Aegeus of Athens.	☐	☑
b	Every year seven young men and women from Athens fight the bulls.	☐	☐
c	There is a monster in a Labyrinth under the palace of Knossos.	☐	☐
d	The monster has the head of a man and the body of a bull.	☐	☐
e	Dedalus teaches only boys at the palace, not girls.	☐	☐
f	Ariadne must marry a prince.	☐	☐
g	Ariadne sends secret messages to Enarus.	☐	☐
h	Icarus tells a servant about Ariadne's secret.	☐	☐

WORD WORK

1 Find twelve more words from Chapter 1 in the wordsquare.

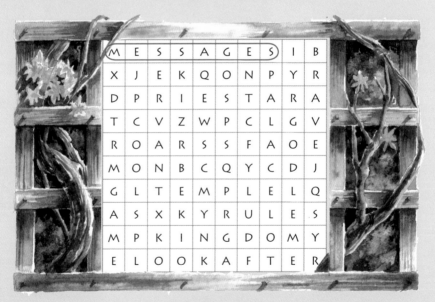

M	E	S	S	A	G	E	S	I	B
X	J	E	K	Q	O	N	P	Y	R
D	P	R	I	E	S	T	A	R	A
T	C	V	Z	W	P	C	L	G	V
R	O	A	R	S	S	F	A	O	E
M	O	N	B	C	Q	Y	C	D	J
G	L	T	E	M	P	L	E	L	Q
A	S	X	K	Y	R	U	L	E	S
M	P	K	I	N	G	D	O	M	Y
E	L	O	O	K	A	F	T	E	R

ACTIVITIES

2 **Use the words from Activity 1 to complete the sentences about the story.**

a Phedra must take ..messages. from her sister to Enarus. She thinks of this as a
new .... to play.

b Minos .... in the .... of Crete.

c Enarus's father works as a .... at the .... of Dionysus.
Dionysus is a very important .... for the people of Crete.

d In the evenings, Ariadne and Enarus meet secretly in the gardens of the king's
.... When the sun has gone down, it is nice and .... there.

e Ariadne can hear the Minotaur when he .... inside the Labyrinth.

f A lot of .... work for King Minos. They help to .... Ariadne
and Phedra.

g Sometimes little boys go inside the Labyrinth. They want to show their friends that
they are very ....

GUESS WHAT

In the next chapter, what does King Minos say to Ariadne? Tick one of the boxes.

a ☐ You must leave Crete tomorrow and never come back.

b ☐ Enarus left Crete yesterday evening. He will never come back.

c ☐ You must go down into the Labyrinth under the palace this evening.

d ☐ Enarus must fight the bulls tomorrow and you must watch him.

Chapter 2 ✦ Messages and dreams

When I arrived, my father was looking out of the window. Without looking at me, he spoke.

'Ariadne,' he said, 'I am not only your father, but also the King. Do you know what that means?'

'Yes, father,' I answered. 'It means that I must **obey** you.'

'Enarus left Crete yesterday evening,' he went on. 'His father and I have agreed that he will never come back to Crete. If he ever tries to come back, not even the High Priest of Dionysus can help him. Do you understand?'

I said nothing.

'Go back to your room,' Minos said quietly. 'And think about what it means to be a princess. You can't do everything that you want to do. Neither can I. Neither can anybody.'

When I got back to my room, I locked the door. I took out all my secret messages from Enarus and I read them again. I remembered all our **meetings** in the gardens. We had so many plans for our life together. Now all our **dreams** and hopes were finished.

I put all Enarus's messages together. Then in the **flame** of the **lamp** that lit my room, I burnt them one by one, and watched my bright dreams change into dark smoke.

Some time later, I heard a knock on my door. It was Phedra. 'Ariadne, sister, come and play with me!' she called through the door. I told her to go away.

In the evening, a servant knocked at my door with some food for me. I told her to go away, too.

Night came, but I couldn't sleep. Through the window I saw the moon and the bright stars in the dark sky. Were they laughing at me – the princess who thought that she could do what she wanted: the little bird in the gold **cage**?

In the morning my mother knocked at my door. 'Ariadne, open this door at once!' she said. I had to open the door for her. She came into my room and looked at me sadly. Another servant with food came into my room after her.

'You must eat, Ariadne,' said my mother.

I ate some of the food to please her.

'Today you can stay in your room,' she said. 'But tomorrow there's a bullfight and your father wants you to be there.'

I said nothing. My mother tried again.

'A handsome, young prince called Theseus has come to the bullfights. He's fighting a very dangerous white bull tomorrow. Everyone says that it's going to be a great fight. I'm sure that you'll enjoy it. I'll send a servant to bring you to the bullfight tomorrow morning.'

After she left, I locked my door again. But in the middle of the afternoon someone pushed a piece of paper under it. 'Is that you, Phedra?' I said angrily. 'Because if it is, you can go away.' But it was silent outside the door. I took the paper and opened it. At once I **recognized** Enarus's writing! My **heart** stopped for a second and I read the note quickly. It said:

I am waiting for you on the island of Naxos.

I opened the door, but there was nobody outside. How did Enarus send me this message? I looked out of the window into the gardens. Again there was nobody. Then I remembered

cage an open box to put birds or animals in

recognize to see something and know what it is

heart this is in your chest; it sends the blood round your body

the words of a song that Phedra often sang: 'Love will find a way.' I laughed aloud.

I burnt this latest note from Enarus too. I didn't want Phedra to find it and give away my secrets again.

'I'll find the way to Naxos, and I'll come to you, Enarus,' I said to myself. I had many **maps** of the sea around Crete and I could find Naxos on one of them, I was sure. Suddenly my hopes, my plans and my dreams were real again. I spent the rest of the day with my maps. My mother was pleased. She thought that I was forgetting Enarus.

The next morning there were crowds and crowds of people at the **bullring** when I arrived. Everyone wanted to watch Theseus's fight with the white bull. I made my way to the special seats where all the important people sat, high above the crowd. My father smiled when he saw me, and he **waved** at the crowd. Then he sat down, and the fight began. Theseus came into the bullring and **bowed** to my father. 'My Enarus is taller and more handsome than this Theseus,' I thought. I smiled as I thought about Enarus. My mother thought that I was smiling at Theseus, so she smiled too. How could my mother understand me so little? She thought that I was like a hungry child with a new tasty fruit in front of me – a child that would soon forget yesterday's apple.

Then the white bull came in. It was big and very angry. Theseus danced very quickly and cleverly around the animal. He was never far from the bull's **horns,** but it couldn't catch him. In the end, it became very tired. At that moment Theseus jumped up and over the bull's horns, and killed it with his knife. Everyone shouted and roared, 'Theseus! Theseus!'

My father jumped up. He was just as excited as the **ordinary** people.

The crowds stopped shouting when they saw my father on his feet. Theseus bowed to him.

map a picture that shows where things are

bullring a round building open to the sky where men fight bulls

wave to move your hand in the air

bow to put down your head in front of someone or something important

horn some animals have two of these long hard white things on their heads for fighting

ordinary not special

'Well done Theseus!' said my father. 'Because you have pleased me, I'll give you what you ask for. What will it be? A hundred gold pieces?'

Theseus looked up at my father.

'I don't want gold, great king,' he answered.

'Then what do you want?' asked Minos, surprised.

'**Freedom**,' said Theseus, 'for me and for all those who have come with me from Athens, freedom not to die in the Labyrinth. We want to go home alive. I also ask for freedom in the future for young people from Athens to live long lives and never to meet the Minotaur!'

freedom being free

ACTIVITIES

READING CHECK

Put these sentences in the correct order. Number them 1–7.

a [ ] _____ doesn't want gold or silver. He asks for his freedom.

b [ ] Ariadne burns all of Enarus's _____ in the flame of a lamp.

c [ ] Theseus bravely fights the _____ and kills it.

d [1] King Minos speaks to Ariadne. He says that _____ has left Crete.

e [ ] _____ goes to the bullring to watch the fight.

f [ ] _____ is pleased with Theseus. He says that Theseus can have what he wants.

g [ ] Someone puts a note under Ariadne's _____. She recognizes the writing.

WORD WORK

1 Find new words from Chapter 2.

a d r e a m — RDMAE

b h _ _ _ _ _ — ROHSN

c o _ _ _ _ _ _ _ _ _ — ADROIRYN

d b _ _ — WOB

e c _ _ _ _ — GAEC

f m _ _ — PMA

g o _ _ _ — BEYO

h w _ _ _ — VAWE

i m _ _ _ _ _ _ _ — EMETNIG

j h _ _ _ _ _ — ERAHT

12

2 Use the words from Activity 1 to complete the sentences.

a Her ... _dream_ ... is to become a doctor when she's older.

b He's very bad at school; he doesn't .... any of his teachers.

c We had a .... yesterday to talk about the new sports centre.

d Oh dear! My bird has escaped from its .... again.

e Her .... is full of love for him.

f Can you find the bus station on the ....?

g Don't forget to .... goodbye when the train leaves.

h When you meet the king, you must .... to him.

i Be careful of that bull – it has very big ....

j This isn't an .... clock – it's a radio too.

GUESS WHAT

What happens in the next chapter?

		Yes	Perhaps	No
a	King Minos gives Theseus his freedom.	☐	☐	☐
b	King Minos is angry and sends Theseus to the Minotaur.	☐	☐	☐
c	Ariadne falls in love with Theseus and secretly marries him.	☐	☐	☐
d	Ariadne plans to sail with Theseus to the island of Naxos.	☐	☐	☐
e	Ariadne tells Dedalus about her secret message from Enarus.	☐	☐	☐
f	Phedra learns about Enarus's message and tells King Minos.	☐	☐	☐

Chapter 3 ⚇ Escape plans

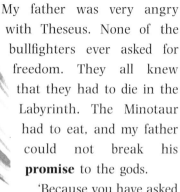

My father was very angry with Theseus. None of the bullfighters ever asked for freedom. They all knew that they had to die in the Labyrinth. The Minotaur had to eat, and my father could not break his **promise** to the gods.

'Because you have asked this thing,' Minos said to Theseus, 'you have made our gods angry. You must go to the Minotaur at once. You have until **midday** to say goodbye to your friends, and then my servants will take you to the Labyrinth.'

The crowds were silent. Theseus walked past the dead bull with his head high. He was going back to the cage under the bullring where they kept all the bullfighters before they went to fight the bulls. Like everyone there, I was sorry that he had to die. Then suddenly I thought of something. Theseus needed to leave Crete and so did I. Perhaps we could help each other. He must know how to sail to Naxos. In my lessons Dedalus often told me that the people of Athens, the Athenians, were very good sailors. How could I **save** him from the monster?

promise
something that you say you will certainly do

midday the middle of the day; twelve o'clock

save to take someone out of danger

14

Then I saw Dedalus. He was talking to my father. Of course! That was it! Dedalus knew how to get out of the Labyrinth. On the way to the palace, I spoke to him. My father was watching us.

'There's a new flower that I want you to look at,' I said loudly. 'I don't know its name. Can you come to the palace gardens and help me?'

Dedalus looked into my eyes. He knew that I wasn't really interested in the names of flowers. He **winked** at me.

'I'll be happy to come with you, princess,' he said.

My father moved away to say something to my mother.

In the gardens Dedalus and I walked far away from all the servants.

'What is it, Ariadne?' he asked quietly. 'I know how sad you are about Enarus. But don't be angry with Phedra. She tried to keep your secret, but she's too young.'

I was surprised.

'Did you know about our meetings?' I asked.

'Of course I did,' said Dedalus, 'but Enarus is a good boy and I saw how you felt about each other. I think that Minos is wrong to say that you must marry a prince. But who am I to **argue** with a king? In time Enarus will forget you, and you'll forget him.'

'We'll never forget,' I answered hotly. 'Enarus is waiting for me to join him on Naxos!'

Now Dedalus was surprised.

'How do you know this?' he asked.

I told him about the message.

'Ah, that's why Enarus sent a letter to Icarus. It had a secret note inside it that he wanted my son to take to you!'

'Right, so Icarus was the messenger. That explains it.'

I told Dedalus about my plan to escape with Theseus.

Dedalus was quiet for a few minutes. Then he spoke.

'It's a good plan,' he said. 'Theseus is a brave prince and

wink to close only one eye quickly

argue to talk angrily with someone when you do not agree with them

his life is important to the gods. I've seen this in the stars. I think that the gods want us to help him. He'll be in the Labyrinth soon and – without someone to help him – the Minotaur will find him quickly. We must get him out soon. There's a secret **passage** into the Labyrinth. If I tell you where it is, you can go and help Theseus. It's dangerous. But you must find him before the Minotaur does.'

'Don't worry about me,' I answered. 'As you yourself said, the daughter of Minos should never be afraid.'

Dedalus smiled again.

'Good girl!' he said. 'Now, Theseus will need a good **sword** to use against the Minotaur. I'll get one now. But how will you both find your way back out of the Labyrinth? I'm too old to run in there with you, and there isn't time to explain the plan of the Labyrinth. You'll need to get back to the secret door at the end of the passage.'

I thought quickly.

'I know,' I said. 'I'll take some strong **thread** from our rooms. I'll **tie** one end of the thread to the door of the Labyrinth as I go in and I'll give the other end to Theseus when I find him. Then we'll only have to follow the thread to find our way back to the secret door. But will it work?'

'I think so,' answered Dedalus. 'And we have no time now to make another plan. Go to your room, Ariadne, and put on some warm clothes. It's cold in the Labyrinth where the sun never shines. Find some strong thread and meet me at the garden door as soon as you can. I'll try to send a message to Theseus, and then I'll come back with the sword. I'll also tell my friends to find a boat for you and Theseus to use later at the **harbour**. You'll need some food and something to drink too. But remember: you mustn't run now. Walk in your usual way and don't look excited. There are servants everywhere who are always watching you. We must be very careful.'

passage a long narrow way

sword a long, sharp knife for fighting

thread a long thin piece of cotton

tie to keep one end of a piece of string in one place by putting it around something

harbour a place where boats can stop safely near land

This time I winked at him. I walked slowly away from
Dedalus to my rooms. He bowed to me, and left by the garden
door. It was difficult to do everything slowly and quietly, but
I don't think that anybody saw anything unusual.

A short time later we met again. I had a big ball of gold
thread in the pocket of my **cloak**.

'Hide this under your cloak,' said Dedalus. I took the sword
from him and did as he said.

'You must use the family door into your father's rooms,'
Dedalus went on. 'The passage that goes to the secret door
into the Labyrinth begins next to the king's bed. If you **lift**
the carpet you'll see a big stone door in the floor next to the
bed. The stone isn't as heavy as it looks: use the metal ring
in the middle of it, and lift it up. You'll see some stairs going
down. Take this lamp with you and go down the stairs.'

Dedalus gave me a small lamp.

cloak you wear
this over your head
and shoulders and
around your arms
and body

lift to move up

'At the bottom of the stairs, take the key that you see on the wall in front of you. You can turn left or right. To enter the Labyrinth you must turn right and walk down a narrow passage. You'll find a small door in front of you. This is the secret door to the Labyrinth. The key will open it.

'If you turn left at the bottom of the stairs, you'll find another passage which leads outside the palace walls. That's how Minos leaves the palace secretly when he needs to. It's also how you and Theseus can leave later tonight.'

'Does Theseus know that I'm coming to help him?'

'No – there was no way to send him a message safely. The servants were on their way to take him to the Labyrinth when I left you. It was too late. You must explain everything when you find him. Go now, Ariadne. Theseus is in great danger. It will not take the monster long to find him.'

Just then, I remembered something important.

'Dedalus,' I said, 'before I go, I'll quickly write a message for my father and leave it in his room. I'll tell him that I found the secret passage myself when I was playing in his rooms as a child. You could die if my father thinks that you've helped me.'

'Thank you, Ariadne,' said Dedalus. 'But don't worry about me. I'm not afraid of your father! Go now and be brave. I know that the gods are with you and Theseus. When you arrive at the harbour, look for a boat with a black sail. It will be ready for your journey. The black sail will be hard for your father's boats to follow in the dark. Go with the gods.'

My good, old friend turned and walked away from me.

Not long after that I was in my father's bedroom. Dedalus was right – I lifted up the stone door in the floor next to the bed quite easily. I quickly wrote the message to my father and left it on his desk. Then I went down the stairs into the dark. I found the key at the bottom of the stairs, and

I turned right. Before long, I came to a small locked door. I opened it with the key in my hand. Then I put my lamp down and I tied the thread to the door **handle**. After that I opened the door quietly and listened. At first I could hear nothing at all. It was very cold and dark. But I knew it was time to go into the Labyrinth. I had to walk away from the door with my gold thread in one hand and my lamp in the other hand. I had to be a brave daughter of Minos.

handle the part of a thing that you hold in your hand; you turn it to open or close a door

READING CHECK

1 Correct the mistakes in these sentences.

a Minos is ~~pleased~~ *angry* with Theseus when he asks for his freedom.

b Ariadne secretly tells Phedra about her plans to escape.

c Dedalus gives Ariadne a letter for Theseus. She hides it under her cloak.

d Theseus knows that Ariadne is coming to help him.

e At the harbour, Ariadne must find a boat with a white sail.

f Ariadne takes a map into the Labyrinth to help her find her way back.

g The secret door into the Labyrinth is under the window in the king's bedroom.

h Ariadne leaves a present for her father on his desk.

WORD WORK

Use the words in the sword to complete the dialogues below.

THESEUS · THREAD · WINKED · PASSAGE · SAVE · MIDDAY · HANDLE · TIE · ARGUE · PROMISE

a 'What are you doing with that long piece of gold ...thread...?'
'I'm trying to .... a card on to this birthday present.'

b 'You won't be late this evening, will you?' 'No, I'll arrive on time, I ....'

c 'I can't swim. If I fall into the river, will you .... me?' 'Yes, of course.'

d How do you open this door?' 'You have to push the .... down hard.'

e 'Do you like your neighbours?' 'No. They always .... and shout a lot.'

f 'Can you .... this box up here?' 'Sorry, I can't. It's too heavy.'

g 'Let's meet at ....' 'How about one o'clock? That's better for me.'

h 'Do you want to walk down that ....?' 'No. It's very dark in there.'

i 'How did you know he was joking?' 'Because he smiled and .... at me.'

GUESS WHAT

What happens to Ariadne in the Labyrinth? Tick one of the boxes.

a ☐ She becomes lost and can't find Theseus in the Labyrinth.

b ☐ She sees the Minotaur and runs out of the Labyrinth alone.

c ☐ She gives Theseus the sword and he uses it to fight the Minotaur.

d ☐ She finds Theseus and helps him to fight the Minotaur.

Chapter 4 ⚘ Into the Labyrinth

I was afraid that my little lamp would suddenly go out and that I would lose myself in the dark. But I knew that I was not alone. Theseus was there somewhere in the Labyrinth with me. I turned right, and then left, and then right again. And I always left some of the gold thread behind me as I went deeper and deeper into the Labyrinth. Suddenly I heard a small noise in front of me. Someone – or something – was moving **towards** me. It was still outside the small circle of light that came from my lamp. Who or what was it?

'Theseus?' I **whispered**. 'I've come to help. I'm a friend.'

At first there was no answer. Perhaps it was the Minotaur. Then I heard Theseus's voice.

'Are you alive? Or are you a **ghost** or a **goddess**?'

'I'm Ariadne, the daughter of Minos,' I answered.

I lifted the light to show my face. He came nearer.

'Yes, I remember your face from the bullfight. You were sitting near your father. It's not a face that a man can easily forget.'

'This is no time for **compliments**,' I replied angrily. 'Are you forgetting the Minotaur? Take this sword which I've brought for you.'

towards nearer

whisper to speak very quietly

ghost a dead person that a living person sees or hears

goddess a woman god

compliment a nice thing that we say to please another person

I took it out from under my cloak and offered it to him.

He looked at me, and said, 'Why is the daughter of King Minos helping me? Is this a good sword or some kind of **trick**?'

'This is no trick,' I answered. 'I need to leave Crete. Can you sail to Naxos?'

'Yes,' he answered. 'If you can help me to leave the Labyrinth and to **rescue** my friends.'

'If you help me to get to Naxos without asking why, I'll help you and your friends,' I said. 'Do you agree?'

Suddenly we heard a terrible roaring behind Theseus.

'I agree, princess,' said Theseus. He took the sword from my hand and turned to **face** the noise.

'Take this, too,' I said. I put the ball of gold thread into his hand. 'When you've killed the monster, follow the thread back to me and then we'll leave the Labyrinth together.'

The roaring was getting louder all the time.

I left Theseus and ran back along the way that was shown by the gold thread to the secret door.

The fight between Theseus and the Minotaur went on for a long time. It was like an **earthquake**. In the end the roaring stopped and Theseus came to me along the way shown by the gold thread. He was very tired.

All he said was 'Shall we go now, princess?'

I took his hand. We went out through the small door, and walked back up the passage to the bottom of the stairs. And then we saw her. Phedra was sitting on the bottom stair.

'Where are you going, Ariadne?' she asked. And she smiled a big smile at Theseus. 'Can I come too?'

'Phedra! How did you get here?' I said.

'Well, you went to your room to put on your cloak. You don't usually wear that heavy cloak in summer time. I thought it was strange. And so I followed you. But tell me, sister, why was the Minotaur roaring so loudly?'

trick to make people believe something that is not true

rescue to save somebody from danger

face to turn your face towards something or someone

earthquake when the ground moves suddenly

I tried to talk to her in a friendly way.

'Phedra,' I said, 'Theseus and I are leaving Crete.'

Phedra looked at Theseus.

'I can understand why Theseus is leaving. But why do you have to go with him. Do you love him?'

'Of course not! You don't understand anything,' I shouted.

Suddenly she started to cry. 'If you try to go now without me, I'll scream, and somebody will come and they'll stop you.' She started to climb up the stairs.

Theseus caught her feet and took her in his arms.

'Can't she come with us?' he asked me.

'But she's so young ... ' I started.

'So were you once, princess,' said Theseus.

I didn't like the way that he called me 'princess'. Phedra just lay in his arms and smiled up at him.

Suddenly I heard **footsteps** above us in my father's room.

'Quick!' I whispered. 'Bring Phedra. This passage leads outside the palace walls.'

'This is so exciting,' whispered Phedra.

'Shh, little princess,' said Theseus quietly.

Phedra looked at him with eyes as big as dinner plates.

In a very short time we reached the bottom of some more stairs. I went up first and Theseus followed, with Phedra in his arms. When we came out into the warm night, I looked around.

'This way to the bullring,' I said.

And so we ran to the cage under the bullring. There the **guards** were sitting asleep around the table in their guard room. There was an empty bottle of drink and some half empty drinking cups on the table. I didn't want my footsteps to wake them so I took my shoes off and walked **barefoot** to take a big key from the hand of one of the guards. Suddenly,

footsteps the noise people make with their feet when they walk

guard someone who stops prisoners from running away

barefoot with nothing on your feet

24

the man cried out, 'Stop, thief!' For one terrible moment I
thought that our escape was over, but then he went on to
laugh in his sleep and said, 'So, you've taken my drink, have
you?' He took his drinking cup in his hand, and went into
a deep sleep once more.

As quietly as I could I walked out of the guard room,
put the key into the lock of the cage door, and opened it.
Theseus's friends kissed my hand in thanks as they came out.
After that Phedra and I, followed by Theseus and his friends
from Athens, ran barefoot through the night to the sea.

ACTIVITIES

READING CHECK

Match the two parts of the sentences.

a Ariadne

b Theseus

c Phedra

d The Minotaur

e The guards

f One of the guards

g Theseus's friends

1 picks up Phedra and carries her.

2 makes a loud noise.

3 are asleep around a table.

4 finds Theseus in the Labyrinth.

5 escape from their cage.

6 looks at Theseus with big eyes.

7 cries out while asleep.

WORD WORK

1 **Find words from Chapter 4 in the Labyrinth.**

2 **Match the words from Activity 1 on page 26 with the definitions.**

a to turn your face to another person. ....face...........

b the noise that a person makes when they walk
on a hard floor. ....

c to save somebody from something dangerous. ....

d with nothing on your feet. ....

e to speak very quietly. ....

f a dead person that a living person can see or hear. ....

g when the ground shakes and moves suddenly. ....

h a nice thing that you say to another person about
their hair, or clothes. ....

i a woman god. ....

j nearer to; on the way to somebody or something. ....

k a clever plan that makes a person believe something
that is not true. ....

GUESS WHAT

What happens in the next chapter? Tick two boxes.

a ☐ Phedra is afraid and wants to go home.

b ☐ King Minos catches Theseus and sends him back to the Minotaur.

c ☐ Ariadne, Theseus and Phedra escape in a boat.

d ☐ There is an earthquake on the island of Crete and many people die.

Chapter 5 ✦ Leaving Crete

As we ran towards the harbour, we heard a lot of noise behind us. Lights came on all over the palace. Everyone was awake there because of the unusual roaring of the Minotaur in the Labyrinth below them.

We ran as fast as we could: I ran faster because Theseus was carrying Phedra in his arms. Theseus's friends ran behind us. When we arrived at the harbour, I looked at all the boats. It was difficult to see the colour of their sails in the dark, but in the end I saw a sail that was a little darker than the others. I climbed onto that boat.

'This way,' I shouted to Theseus.

'This way,' shouted Theseus to his friends.

Suddenly I saw moving lights on the hill.

'Hurry, Theseus,' I shouted. 'They're coming after us.'

Theseus jumped into the boat. His friends followed.

'**Untie** the boat,' he called to one of his friends, putting Phedra down in the boat. 'Luckily there's some wind to take us out to sea. But it's a strange, hot wind for this time of year.'

The lights were getting close to the harbour.

'This is no time to talk about the weather,' I said.

'From now on,' said Theseus, 'the weather is the most important thing for us. You'll have to learn that.'

The wind found our black sail and we started to move slowly out of the harbour.

'Can't we go any faster?' I shouted to the Athenians as a group of Cretan men arrived at the harbour. They were palace servants – some of my father's fastest runners. They started to look at all the boats.

'They haven't seen us yet,' said Theseus, watching them. 'This black sail was a good **idea**, princess.'

'Thank you for the compliment but it really wasn't my

untie to take off ropes that tie someone or something

idea a plan or a new thought

idea . . . ' I started to explain.

But I couldn't finish. Suddenly all the cats and dogs in the streets near the harbour started to **howl**. It was a terrible noise. Phedra screamed. My father's men now saw us in the harbour. Some of them jumped into the water and started to swim towards us. But they didn't get far. There was a big roar from under the ground. The little houses round the harbour started to move. Some palace servants fell into the sea from the harbour wall. Then a big **wave** picked up our boat and carried us out of the harbour. Suddenly we were moving very fast away from the **land**.

'An earthquake,' shouted Theseus. 'Don't worry. My father Poseidon, the god of the sea, will look after us.'

I found Phedra's hand and held it strongly. Theseus took my other hand. The other Athenians quickly took down the sail and held on to the sides of our boat as it ran out to sea. I don't know how long we travelled on that wave.

Then suddenly everything was quiet. The wave dropped our boat and moved on. The wind stopped. We were a long way from land. But we could still hear screams and shouts for help coming from our island home. I smelled smoke.

'Ariadne, look!' shouted Phedra.

She was looking at our palace. But it wasn't there any more. There was just a great ball of fire at the top of the hill. The flames jumped high into the night sky.

'What about Icarus?' screamed Phedra. 'And Dedalus, and mother and father?'

'Dedalus is an **inventor**. He'll have something ready that will save them,' I said.

'But many people on the island will die,' said Theseus. 'The gods are angry with Crete. This is a terrible earthquake. I've never seen a bigger one.'

For once he was not smiling. Phedra started to cry.

'There's nothing that we can do to save them I'm afraid,

howl to make a long, loud, high crying noise like a wolf or a dog

wave a line of water that moves across the top of the sea

land the part of the earth that is not the sea

inventor someone who thinks of new or better things

29

little princess,' said Theseus kindly. 'The game isn't so funny any more, is it? The best thing that you can do is to sleep a little. I know how tired you must be. Lie down here.'

And he made a bed for Phedra with his cloak.

Phedra obeyed him, and she soon fell asleep. I was surprised. She never obeyed me.

But Theseus and his friends were too busy to sleep. They started to put up the sail on our boat once more. They were happily thinking of going back home to Athens. I was sadly watching my home country in terrible trouble. There were fires everywhere, not only at the palace. I could see big waves around the island, too. They were washing away poor people's houses near the sea. We were far away now, but I could still hear the screams that were brought to me by the wind.

'What have we done to make the gods so angry?' I cried. 'Is this because Theseus has killed the Minotaur? Or because my father did not give Theseus what he asked for?'

Theseus said nothing, but he came over and stood by my side.

When the sun came up, a soft cool wind started. Our boat moved on away from Crete until we could no longer see land. Phedra woke up.

'I'm hungry,' she said.

'That's funny,' said Theseus. 'So am I. Luckily my men have found some bread, chicken and fruit here in the boat – and some bottles of water. Your clever sister has thought of everything.'

I was too tired to explain about Dedalus.

Theseus looked into my face.

'You need to sleep, Ariadne,' he said. 'Lie down under my cloak and I'll look after Phedra.'

I was too tired to argue. I lay down in the bottom of the boat and fell asleep.

READING CHECK

Choose the right words to finish the sentences.

a Everyone in the palace hears . . .
1 ☐ the noise of the earthquake.
2 ☑ the Minotaur's roars.
3 ☐ Theseus's loud footsteps.

b . . . follow Theseus, Ariadne and Phedra.
1 ☐ Some of the palace servants
2 ☐ King Minos and his guards
3 ☐ Dedalus and Icarus

c Theseus, Ariadne and Phedra find . . .
1 ☐ the boat with the white sail.
2 ☐ the boat with the blue sail.
3 ☐ the boat with the black sail.

d Suddenly all the . . . begin to howl.
1 ☐ babies
2 ☐ cats and dogs
3 ☐ gods and goddesses

e A large . . . pushes the boat out to sea.
1 ☐ sailor
2 ☐ fish
3 ☐ wave

f There is a . . .
1 ☐ terrible earthquake on the island.
2 ☐ cold wind from the north.
3 ☐ sudden storm over the palace.

g The king's palace is now . . .
1 ☐ full of water.
2 ☐ on fire.
3 ☐ dark and empty.

h Phedra . . .
1 ☐ shouts at and hits Ariadne.
2 ☐ tries to swim back to Crete.
3 ☐ goes to sleep on the boat.

WORD WORK

Find words in the sails to complete the sentences.

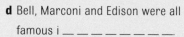

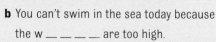
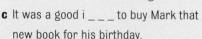

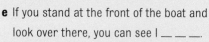

a It was time to leave the harbour so we started to u n t i e the boat.

b You can't swim in the sea today because the w _ _ _ _ are too high.

c It was a good i _ _ _ to buy Mark that new book for his birthday.

d Bell, Marconi and Edison were all famous i _ _ _ _ _ _ _ _ _.

e If you stand at the front of the boat and look over there, you can see l _ _ _.

f When our dog is afraid, it always starts to h _ _ _.

GUESS WHAT

What happens in the next chapter? Tick the boxes.

a Theseus . . .

  1 ☐ goes immediately to Athens with Ariadne and Phedra.

  2 ☐ takes Ariadne and Phedra to the island of Naxos.

b Ariadne . . .

  1 ☐ marries Theseus on the island of Kalliste.

  2 ☐ keeps her plan to meet Enarus a secret.

c Phedra . . .

  1 ☐ wants to go back to her mother and father.

  2 ☐ laughs and talks with Theseus on the boat.

Chapter 6 ✦ On the boat

When I woke up again, it was late afternoon. The boat was sailing towards the north. Theseus's friends were looking after it, and Theseus and Phedra were sitting at the back. They were talking together quietly. Phedra laughed at something Theseus said, and then she saw me.

'You've been asleep a long time!' she said.

'Your sister was very tired,' said Theseus. 'Would you like something to eat, Ariadne?'

'Where are we?' I asked while I ate and drank.

'We're sailing towards Kalliste,' he answered, 'but we're only about half way there. Luckily we've got enough food and water for a few days. And the wind is good for us.'

I thought about my maps. Naxos was north of Kalliste. I was on my way to Enarus!

'Thank you for looking after Phedra,' I said to Theseus.

He gave me more bread, chicken, and water.

'Eat as much as you like,' he said. 'There are shops in Kalliste where we can buy more food.'

'But we haven't any money, have we?' said Phedra.

'I'm still wearing my gold rings and **necklaces**,' I told her. 'We can sell them for money.'

'And I hid some money in a secret pocket in my cloak when I arrived in Crete,' said Theseus. 'We have enough to pay for everything we need.'

'I hope that we're not taking you and your friends too far from Athens,' I said. 'You've been in Crete a long time.'

'Yes,' he said. 'I'm afraid that my father, King Aegeus, thinks that I'm dead. But – Naxos is on the way to Athens. I can sail home quickly from there.'

'But you said that your father was Poseidon, the god of the sea, didn't you?' said Phedra suddenly.

'You remember everything, don't you?' said Theseus.

'So how can you have two fathers at the same time?' asked Phedra.

'Well, if you like, you can say that I have one father in this world and one father in the world after death. My father in the world after death is Poseidon. My father in this world is Aegeus, the king of Athens. He's waiting for me to come back from Crete and to rule our kingdom after he dies. That's why I must go home quickly. I don't want him to think that I'm dead. It could break his heart.'

'Then why don't we go to Athens now?' asked Phedra.

'Ask Ariadne,' said Theseus. 'She wants to go to Naxos.'

'I'll tell you when we arrive,' I answered.

I didn't want to **share** any more of my secrets with Phedra. And I wasn't sure about Enarus's last message – perhaps it wasn't really from him, or perhaps he wasn't on Naxos any longer. But I secretly **clung** to the idea of seeing him soon.

necklace you wear this around your neck

share to take a part of something yourself and to give the other part to another person or people

cling (*past* **clung**) to hold strongly

When Theseus slept, we helped the other Athenians to look after the boat. There was a soft cool wind, so we didn't find it difficult. When Theseus woke up, we slept.

The next day at breakfast Theseus looked at the sail.

'I must remember to change that before I get back to Athens,' he said. 'I told my father that I'd come home as soon as I could. But I said that a black sail would mean bad news – my death. I never thought that a black sail could be useful in a different way – like this one has been for us.'

Then Theseus looked at me strangely.

'Where will you go after Naxos?' he asked.

'Oh – I don't know,' I answered.

'What a beautiful, **secretive** princess you are,' said Theseus.

'What Phedra and I do next is nothing to do with you,' I said coldly.

'I'm sorry to hear that,' said Theseus. 'I thought that you could both come with me to Athens. I know that my father would be happy to meet the daughters of King Minos.'

'That's a good idea!' cried Phedra. 'Let's go to Athens.'

'It's the first place that they'll look for us,' I said. 'They'll know by now that we left with Theseus.'

'It will be hard to hide from King Minos for ever,' said Theseus quietly. He looked **tense** and angry. Did he really think that I wanted to be with him?

'Don't worry about us,' I said. 'We'll be fine.'

But I had no plan if we didn't find Enarus on Naxos.

I looked out over the sea. 'Please be there, Enarus,' I thought.

I fell asleep again in the hot afternoon sun. But I woke up suddenly when Phedra shouted: 'I can see land!'

It was Kalliste. Theseus took the boat into the harbour. There we bought some food and more water. Theseus wanted to stay in Kalliste for a while, where he knew some people, but I didn't want to wait.

secretive keeping secrets

tense worried; not restful and happy

'We must get to Naxos as
soon as we can,' I said.

'I can't understand you,' he said. 'Naxos isn't
a very interesting island.'

'You made a promise,' I shouted. 'Have you forgotten
the Labyrinth so quickly?'

His face went white.

'Get into the boat – now!' he shouted to Phedra who was
playing on the harbour wall, and he called to his friends.
'Move it! We're leaving – at once!'

'Why are you so cross with me?' howled Phedra.

'I'm not,' he said. I knew that he was cross with me.

We sailed on without Theseus saying another word. It
wasn't a very comfortable journey. We all felt tense. At last
we saw a big, new island in front of us.

'Ariadne, this is Naxos,' said Theseus.

READING CHECK

1 Choose the correct words to complete the sentences.

a Ariadne goes to sleep for a short / long time.

b When Ariadne wakes up, Theseus and Phedra are talking quietly / arguing loudly .

c Theseus's father in the world after death is Poseidon, god of the wind / sea .

d A black sail on the boat will tell King Aegeus that his son Theseus is dead / ill .

e Theseus wants to take Ariadne and Phedra back to Crete / Athens .

f Ariadne tells / doesn't tell Theseus and Phedra about Enarus.

g Theseus thinks that Ariadne is / isn't a very open person.

h Ariadne, Theseus and Phedra stay on the island of Kalliste for a few hours / days .

i When the boat sails from Kalliste to Naxos, Theseus doesn't sit with / talk to Ariadne.

2 Complete the sentences with the pictures.

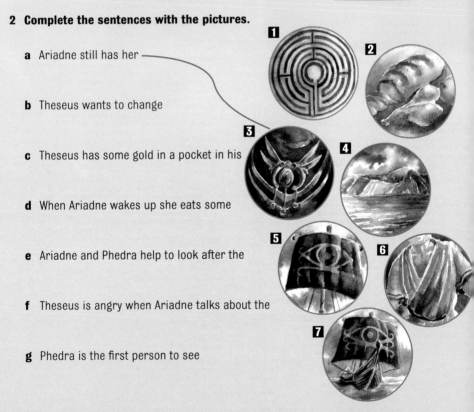

a Ariadne still has her

b Theseus wants to change

c Theseus has some gold in a pocket in his

d When Ariadne wakes up she eats some

e Ariadne and Phedra help to look after the

f Theseus is angry when Ariadne talks about the

g Phedra is the first person to see

WORD WORK

Complete the words to make sentences. All the words come from Chapter 6.

a He seems very _t e n s e_ today. I think he's worried about something.

b Rose felt afraid on her first day at school and c __ u __ g to her mother.

c There was only one cake left, so we agreed to __ h __ r __ it.

d He's a very __ e __ r __ t __ v __ person. He never tells me anything.

e We arrived late at the station and we __ __ m __ __ t missed the train.

f She was wearing a beautiful gold __ e __ __ l __ c __ .

GUESS WHAT

Who or what does Ariadne find on the island of Naxos? Tick one box.

a ☐ Enarus's dead body.

b ☐ Enarus.

c ☐ A secret message from Enarus.

d ☐ King Minos and his guards.

Chapter 7 ⚘ Arriving on Naxos

The harbour on Naxos was busy when we arrived. Theseus said to us:

'I'm going with my friends to buy a new white sail for the boat. Why don't you two look around the town? I'll meet you back here at midday. Then perhaps you can explain your mystery, Ariadne. I'm not going to leave you here until I know that you're safe.'

I agreed. I wanted to get away quickly. I walked through the busy streets with Phedra behind me.

'Wait for me!' she shouted. 'Where are we going?'

'We must find the temple of Dionysus,' I said. I knew that this was the best place to look for Enarus. His father had many friends who were priests of Dionysus on other islands.

'Why?' shouted Phedra, as I pushed through the crowds.

I had to tell her.

'I'm looking for Enarus,' I shouted back. 'Hurry up, Phedra.'

'Enarus?' she answered. 'Is he here?'

'I hope so,' I said. 'He sent me a message from Naxos and asked me to come here.'

Phedra put her hand on my arm.

'You love him, don't you?' she asked.

'I've always loved him,' I said. 'But I didn't know how much until father sent him away. I couldn't stay in Crete after he left.'

Phedra **nodded** like a little, old lady.

'I know what you mean,' she said, 'because I love Theseus.'

'Oh, come on Phedra,' I said. 'You're too young to understand about love between a man and a woman.'

'I know that I'm young,' she said, 'but I love him.'

'Well,' I said, 'we haven't got time to talk about it now.

nod to move your
head up and down

40

Let's go and find Enarus.'

'All right,' she said, happy again.

When we arrived at the temple, I looked around. There were a few priests, but I couldn't see Enarus. Then I saw a small garden beside the temple. Someone was sitting there alone, under an orange tree.

'Phedra, he's here,' I said. I was so happy that I just stood and looked at him. But Phedra ran towards him.

'Enarus, we're here!' she shouted.

He turned around and saw me. His sudden smile was like the sun in the morning. I ran into his arms.

'Ariadne, how did you get away so quickly? What about Minos? Are you all right?' he asked.

'We're fine,' I said. 'Somebody brought us here.'

'It's so wonderful to see you – and you too, Phedra,' he laughed, as she started to pull his hand.

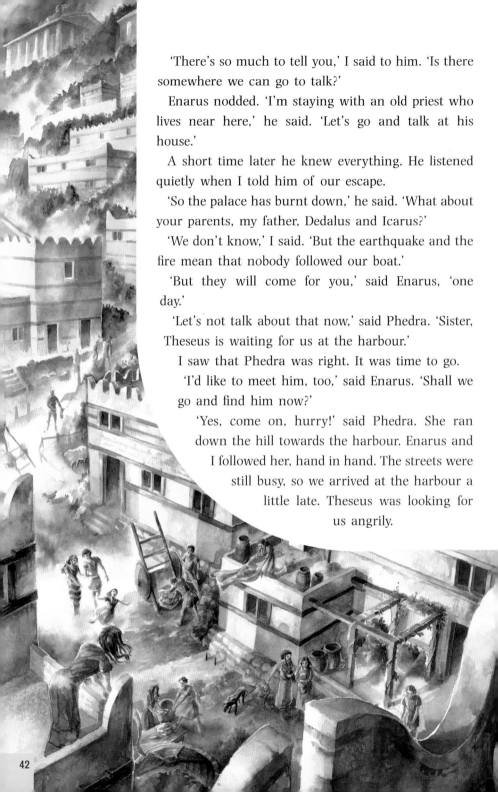

'There's so much to tell you,' I said to him. 'Is there somewhere we can go to talk?'

Enarus nodded. 'I'm staying with an old priest who lives near here,' he said. 'Let's go and talk at his house.'

A short time later he knew everything. He listened quietly when I told him of our escape.

'So the palace has burnt down,' he said. 'What about your parents, my father, Dedalus and Icarus?'

'We don't know,' I said. 'But the earthquake and the fire mean that nobody followed our boat.'

'But they will come for you,' said Enarus, 'one day.'

'Let's not talk about that now,' said Phedra. 'Sister, Theseus is waiting for us at the harbour.'

I saw that Phedra was right. It was time to go.

'I'd like to meet him, too,' said Enarus. 'Shall we go and find him now?'

'Yes, come on, hurry!' said Phedra. She ran down the hill towards the harbour. Enarus and I followed her, hand in hand. The streets were still busy, so we arrived at the harbour a little late. Theseus was looking for us angrily.

Phedra ran up to him.

'Here we are!' she said happily. Theseus looked over her head and saw me with Enarus. His face changed. Suddenly he looked more unhappy than angry.

Enarus walked straight up to him and bowed politely. 'Prince Theseus,' he said. 'I'm very happy to meet you. My name is Enarus and I've known Ariadne and Phedra for many years. I want to thank you for bringing them to me.'

He smiled at Theseus.

'Ariadne means the world to me and she always has done. I'll look after her and Phedra from now on.'

'So, this is your mystery, princess,' said Theseus, 'You're **certainly** a secretive young woman!'

'You must be hungry and tired after your journey,' said Enarus. 'Would you and your Athenian friends like to eat with us at the temple before you leave? Ariadne has told me that you need to sail to Athens before long.'

'Very well,' said Theseus. I could see that it was difficult for him to say 'no' to Enarus.

'I'll tell the priests that we have a most important visitor,' said Enarus. 'You'll soon be famous in Naxos, Theseus, for killing the terrible Minotaur.'

Phedra's eyes opened wide.

'Are you going to be famous?' she asked Theseus.

'In Athens I'm famous already,' he answered.

'Can I come to Athens with you?' asked Phedra.

'Phedra,' I said, 'Just be quiet for once!'

'It's all right,' said Theseus. 'Princess Phedra will be welcome in Athens one day.'

So together with Theseus and the other Athenians we left the harbour and went to eat with the priests. They gave us all a wonderful meal and then somewhere to sleep. Enarus didn't tell the priests that Phedra and I were princesses from Crete. He just said that we were friends. But the priests knew

certainly for sure

who Theseus was, and they were a little afraid of him as the son of King Aegeus. I understood that he was a very important prince in that part of the world. Theseus said that he wanted to leave early the next morning. So we agreed to say goodbye at the harbour as soon as the sun came up.

When we got up, Phedra was unusually quiet.

'What is it?' I asked her, as we dressed in our room.

'I want to go to Athens with Theseus,' she said. 'You don't want me to stay here with you and Enarus, do you?'

'Well, of course I thought that you would want to stay with us.'

'Well, I don't,' said my strange little sister. 'I want to go with Theseus and then I want to go home again to see mother and father. You don't want to see them, do you?'

'Phedra,' I said. 'I love Enarus, but father will never **allow** me to marry him because he's not a prince. What can I do?'

'You can stay here with him,' said Phedra. 'I won't tell anyone.'

'It's a big secret,' I said to her. 'Can you keep it?'

'If you allow me to go with Theseus, I'll keep it,' she said. I could see that she meant it. She was also right. I could never see my parents again. I had to **disappear**.

'We must talk to Theseus and Enarus about this,' I said. 'We must all agree. There are four people in this secret. And perhaps Theseus won't agree.'

When we left our room, Enarus was waiting.

'Theseus is already at the harbour,' he said. 'He left some time ago.'

On the way to the harbour, we told Enarus about Phedra's idea. Enarus looked at me carefully.

'Do you understand what this means, Ariadne? You won't be a princess any more. And you'll never see Crete or your family again. I can't ask you to do this for me.'

allow to say that someone can do something

disappear to go away suddenly

I looked at the women in the street so early in the morning. Some were going to the harbour to say goodbye to their husbands who – it was **clear** – went fishing every day. Others were going to buy fish from the early morning boats. Some were already **cleaning** their houses in the early light. They were talking together or singing as they worked.

'Look at those women. They aren't unhappy,' I said to Enarus. 'They're busy, but in a strange way they're free. I've never been free.'

We arrived at the harbour. Theseus was cleaning the boat. His Athenian friends were helping him.

'We'll soon be going on our way to Athens,' he said.

'Have you got room for me on the boat?' asked Phedra.

'What?!' said Theseus.

Enarus and I explained our plan to him.

'You know what people will say, Ariadne,' he said. 'They'll say that you sailed away with me because you loved me. Then they'll say that I left you here because I didn't love you. What do you think of that?'

'People can think what they like, Theseus,' I said. 'I have my Enarus. That's the only important thing.'

He didn't like what I said.

'Right then, Phedra,' he said. 'It's time to go.'

Phedra jumped into the boat and clung to Theseus's arm.

'Goodbye Ariadne, goodbye Enarus! Be happy!' she shouted.

'Good luck to you both!' I shouted back.

clear easy to understand

clean to stop something being dirty

READING CHECK

1 Who says what? Mark the sentences A (Ariadne), P (Phedra), T (Theseus) or E (Enarus).

a 'I've always loved him.' ...A.

b 'I know what you mean, because I love Theseus.' ......

c 'But they will come for you, one day.' ......

d 'You don't want me to stay here with you and Enarus, do you?' ......

e 'You're certainly a secretive young woman.' ......

f 'In Athens I'm famous already.' ......

g 'It's a big secret. Can you keep it?' ......

h 'I can't ask you to do this for me.' ......

i 'Have you got room for me on the boat?' ......

j 'Then they'll say that I left you here because I didn't love you.' ......

k 'People can think what they like.' ......

2 Correct seven more mistakes in the story.

Naxos

When Theseus, Phedra and Ariadne arrive on the island of ~~Kalliste~~, Theseus goes to buy a new black sail. Ariadne starts to look for Enarus and takes Phedra with her to the temple of Poseidon. They find Enarus sitting alone under a lemon tree in the garden.

Ariadne, Phedra and Enarus walk down the hill to the river to meet Theseus and his friends. Enarus invites them to dance with the priests that evening at the temple.

The next morning Ariadne decides to stay on the island of Naxos and become just an ordinary princess. Phedra asks to go to Crete with Theseus on his boat and he agrees. Phedra waves goodbye as they sail away from the island.

WORD WORK

Use the words in the temple to complete the sentences.

a I ..*cleaned*... the car because it was so dirty.

b If you understand and agree, ... your head.

c He's .... the fastest runner in the whole school. No one is as fast as him.

d Her parents .... her to go out every Saturday night.

e Our dog has .... and we can't find it.

f She didn't understand the teacher's question because it wasn't very ....

GUESS WHAT

What happens in the next chapter? Tick the boxes.

a On the island of Naxos, Ariadne is . . .

1 ☐ free and happy.   **2** ☐ angry and unhappy.   **3** ☐ ill and poor.

b When Theseus arrives in Athens, he . . .

1 ☐ becomes king.   **2** ☐ fights King Minos.   **3** ☐ sends Phedra home to Crete.

Chapter 8 ◍ Sofia's life

beyond on the far side of something

horizon where we see the sky and sea meet far away from us

point to show where something is with your finger

On that morning so long ago, Theseus sailed away quickly. He never looked back. But Phedra waved at us for as long as she could see us. Enarus and I stood and watched the boat. We could easily see the black sail against the blue sky.

Suddenly I remembered.

'The black sail,' I cried. 'Theseus wanted to change it before he left.'

I told Enarus why. Soon after that, a man arrived at the harbour with a new, white sail.

'Where's the prince from Athens?' he asked everybody.

'He's gone,' I said. Theseus's boat was disappearing fast **beyond** the **horizon**. I **pointed** to it. 'That's his boat. You can just see the black sail.'

'But he asked me to make this new sail,' said the man. 'And he hasn't paid me for it.' He looked very angry.

'How much is it?' I asked the man. 'Can I pay you with this gold necklace?' I untied my necklace and took it from my neck to show it to him.

'That's **solid** gold, isn't it?' he said. I nodded. 'Then it's too much for one sail,' he went on.

'Then give me a small boat, too,' I said. Enarus looked worried, but I explained. 'We don't need gold here, but perhaps we'll need a boat for fishing.'

I smiled at the man. 'Is that all right?'

'Oh yes,' he answered. 'Come with me.'

Enarus and I followed the man to his shop.

Enarus and I were married in the temple of Dionysus a week after Theseus and Phedra left. I changed my name to Sofia. That means '**wise** one' in Greek. I was sure that I was wise to choose a life with Enarus and to leave my old life behind me. I had to follow my heart. Nobody in Naxos ever knew who I really was. About a month after we married, a boat came from Crete. They were looking for me and Phedra. Someone told them that Theseus was on the way to Athens with some Athenian friends. No one recognized me in my ordinary clothes. The Cretans left for Athens. I didn't know what Theseus and Phedra would say to them there, but I knew that they wouldn't tell the **truth** about me and Enarus.

After a year people stopped asking questions about Princess Ariadne. She just disappeared – became a ghost. But Sofia was alive and safe, and soon she was **pregnant**. Her baby, when it came, was a beautiful boy. She called him Orestes. That means 'mountain'. Orestes grew to be tall and handsome like his father. Two years later, Sofia became pregnant again. This time she had a girl. She called her second child Artemisia. That means 'moon'. Artemisia was a wild child who often ran barefoot into the fields to play with the animals. Some people on Naxos pointed their fingers at me and said that I was a bad mother because I allowed my daughter to be too free. But I wanted my children to be happy when they were

solid with no other things in it

wise intelligent, clever

truth what is true

pregnant when a woman is waiting for a child

young. I don't think that they ever had a teacher as good as Dedalus was to me, but Enarus and I taught them many things that you can't learn at school. We taught them that money isn't as important as freedom, and that shared love is more important than anything. When Artemisia told me that she wanted to be like a princess in one of the old stories, I asked her if she thought that princesses were happy. She said, 'I'm not sure.' I told her, 'I don't think that kings and **queens** and princes and princesses have time to be happy.' She thought hard. For a minute, she almost looked like Phedra when I last saw her in the harbour with Theseus.

'But I <u>would</u> like some servants,' she said.

Not much news **reaches** Naxos from other countries beyond the islands around us. But one day, not long after Theseus left, we learnt that he was now king of Athens. When we heard about the death of his father, Aegeus, I was very sorry. As soon as he saw the black sail on Theseus's boat, he jumped from a mountain near Athens into the sea – now called the Aegean after him. What a terrible thing to happen on the day that Theseus reached his **homeland**! Some time later, I heard that Theseus was now married to a tall, strong woman – Queen Hippolyta, and that they had a son, Hippolytus. Then, after some years, more news reached us from Athens. Hippolyta was dead and Theseus had a new wife – a beautiful young princess from Crete. I understood then that Phedra must be Theseus's new wife. I remembered her words to me that morning in Naxos so many years earlier: 'I love him.' I was surprised because he was so much older than her, but I hoped they would be happy together. Sadly last year the news came that Phedra was dead. People said that she and Theseus argued, often about Hippolytus, and in the end she killed herself. I saw her ghost in my dreams just before the news came. My poor little sister: she **deserved** a better life.

queen the wife of a king

reach to arrive in a place after travelling for some time

homeland the country that someone comes from

deserve to get what is right for you

My life as Sofia, after twenty years on Naxos, is a happy one. And I'm happy for my children too! Their lives will certainly be much easier than Phedra's. Orestes already loves a girl here in Naxos and I think that they will marry soon. Lots of boys like Artemisia, but she hasn't fallen in love with any of them yet. When she's ready, she can decide who to marry and Enarus and I won't stop her.

I sometimes think about Theseus. Has his life been happy? He has clearly ruled his kingdom well: Athens is now famous. After the earthquake, Crete became weak and Athens is now much stronger than my homeland. Perhaps Theseus learned some lessons from his time in Crete. He saw how my father ruled his kingdom and he decided not to make the same mistakes. But I don't forget the good things. He brought me safely here to Naxos and he's kept his promise. So I ask the goddesses Hera, Athena, and Aphrodite to look after him when I go to the temple. He deserves their help. Theseus and I will never meet again, but I haven't forgotten him, and I feel sure that he hasn't forgotten me.

READING CHECK

Are these sentences true or false? Tick the boxes.

		True	False
a	Theseus puts the white sail up on his boat.	☐	☑
b	Enarus marries Ariadne at the temple of Dionysus.	☐	☐
c	Ariadne changes her name to Artemesia.	☐	☐
d	Everybody on Naxos knows who Ariadne really is.	☐	☐
e	Some Cretans come to look for Ariadne but they leave.	☐	☐
f	Enarus and Ariadne have two children.	☐	☐
g	Artemesia is a wise and quiet girl who stays at home.	☐	☐
h	Phedra is happily married to Theseus for many years.	☐	☐
i	Athens is now much stronger than Crete.	☐	☐
j	Ariadne leads a sad and lonely life on Naxos.	☐	☐

WORD WORK

1 Find words from Chapter 8 in these sentences and complete the puzzle on page 53.

a Ariadne *onipst* to the black sail on Theseus's boat.

b The news about Phedra doesn't *ercah* Naxos for a long time.

c Theseus's boat disappears quickly over the *ronhozi* towards Athens.

d Phedra doesn't tell anybody the *thrut* about Ariadne and Enarus.

e Theseus wants to go back to his *onldmaeh* to see his father.

f Phedra is very unhappy; she *eervseds* a better life, thinks Ariadne.

g Ariadne becomes *rgetpnan* and has a baby daughter.

h Ariadne buys a boat and a sail with her *sldoi* gold necklace.

i Athens lies some way across the sea *dbyeno* the island of Naxos.

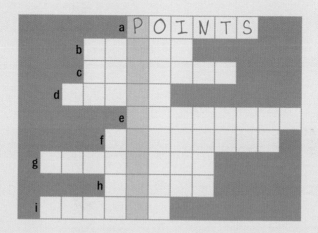

a P O I N T S
b
c
d
e
f
g
h
i

Read the blue squares above and find the name of this old building in Athens.

The P _ _ _ _ _ _ _ _.

PROJECT A   *Writing a note*

1   Look at Enarus's note to Ariadne.

> Ariadne
> Not sure if note will reach you, but really wanted to write immediately.
> Waiting for you on Naxos. Very small island — not much to do here.
> Working as priest in Temple of Dionysus. Other priests friendly.
> Journey here very long. Having terrible time without you. Come soon.
> Love
> Enarus

Notes are different from letters. We often miss out less important words. Write the words in the box in the correct places in the note to change it into a letter below.

a	a	and there's	are	dear	I	I'm	I'm	I'm	I'm	it's a
lots of	please	the	the	the	the island of		this		was	

> .... Ariadne
> .... not sure if .... note will reach you, but
> .... really wanted to write immediately. ....
> waiting for you on .... Naxos. .... very small
> island — .... not much to do here. .... working
> as .... priest in .... Temple of Dionysus.
> .... other priests .... friendly. ....
> journey here................. very long. .... having
> .... terrible time without you. .... come soon.
> .... love,
> Enarus

2 **Read Phedra's letter to Ariadne. Cross out the words that could be missed out in a note.**

> Dear Ariadne
>
> I'm not sure if this note will reach you but I wanted to tell you my news! I'm getting married next month to Theseus in his capital Athens. It's a very big city – and there's lots to do here. I'm really enjoying myself. Theseus's son Hippolytus is very nice. The journey here was long and tiring. I'm writing to ask you to the wedding. Please come if you can. With lots of love
>
> Phedra

3 **Write a note back from Ariadne to Phedra. Miss out words that are not necessary.**

PROJECTS

PROJECT B   *Telling a story*

1 What happened to Dedalus and Icarus after the end of *Ariadne's Story*? Use the words in the box to complete their story.

at once	because	but	in the end	so	soon
suddenly	then	until	when	while	

(a)................. King Minos learned about Theseus, Ariadne and Phedra, he became very angry. 'Bring me, Dedalus (b) ....!' he cried. 'I know that he helped them to escape!'

King Minos sent Dedalus and his son, Icarus, into the dark Labyrinth with no food or water. They (c) .... became hungry and thirsty. (d)................. Dedalus was a clever man. He started to think of how to escape (e).................. he was sitting in the dark.

Years before, Dedalus helped to build the Labyrinth, (f)................. he knew it well. In its passages he found some old feathers and beeswax. With these he made two pairs of wings — for himself and Icarus.

Dedalus taught Icarus to fly. 'Be careful,' he said. 'Don't fly down too near the sea (g) .... the feathers on your wings will get wet in the water and too heavy to fly. And don't fly up too near the sun or the wax on the wings will get hot and they'll break.'

That afternoon Dedalus and Icarus put on their wings. (h)................. they climbed quietly out of the Labyrinth. They flew up into the air. 'Look at me!' cried Icarus. 'Remember what I said!' shouted Dedalus.

Icarus didn't remember. He flew up towards the sun happily (i)................. it melted the wax on his wings. He (j)................. fell down into the sea! Icarus tried to swim with his wet wings without any luck. (k)................. the heavy feathers pulled him down into the water where he died.

2 **Read the story of *King Midas and the Golden Touch*. Match a picture with each sentence.**

a Every night King Midas counted all the gold in his palace. He wasn't happy. He dreamed of having more.

b One night a hungry satyr – Silenus – came to his palace. Midas gave him dinner.

c The god Dionysus arrived. Midas and Silenus were eating.

d Dionysius was pleased with Midas. Silenus was his friend.

e The god smiled at Midas. He said, 'Ask me for anything. I'll give it to you as a present.'

f King Midas remembered his dream. 'I want everything that I touch to change into gold!' he said.

g Midas was happy with his present. He touched his daughter. She changed into gold.

h Midas asked Dionysius for help. The god told him to wash in the river. He did this. The 'Golden Touch' left him.

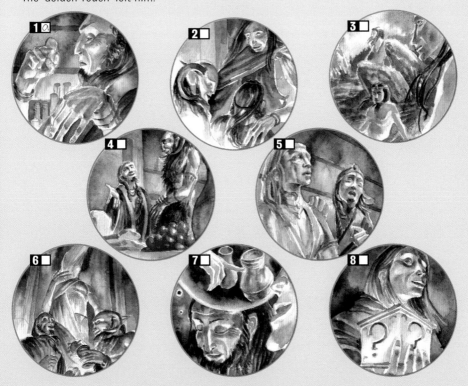

PROJECTS

3 **Write the story of *King Midas and the Golden Touch*. Use the sentences from Activity 2 and the words in brackets.**

a (because, but) _____

_____

b (so) _____

_____

c (while) _____

_____

d (because) _____

_____

e (then) _____

_____

f (suddenly, at once) _____

_____

g (until, and) _____

_____

h (in the end, when, soon) _____

_____

4 **Find another old story. Rewrite it using the words from 3. Find or draw a picture – or some pictures – to help tell the story.**

Choosing Athena or Poseidon

The Judgement of Paris

GRAMMAR

GRAMMAR CHECK

Past Continuous and Past Simple with when

We use the Past Continuous to talk about longer actions in the past, and the Past Simple to talk about shorter actions in the past.

Ariadne and Enarus were talking in the garden. The Minotaur was roaring.

Ariadne went to her room. She sat down.

We use the time expression when to show the relationship between two actions in the past. We use the Past Continuous for the longer action and the Past Simple for the shorter action. If the when clause comes first, we put a comma after it.

Ariadne and Enarus were laughing together when King Minos arrived.

1 **Choose the correct word or words to complete the sentences.**

a When we **were coming/came** out of the passage, she **was waiting/waited** for us.

b Ariadne **wasn't studying/studied** when somebody **was leaving/left** the note.

c Ariadne **was walking/walked** away when Dedalus **was bowing/bowed**.

d They **were sailing/sailed** away when they **were hearing/heard** the earthquake.

e When Ariadne **was finding/found** Enarus he **was sitting/sat** under an orange tree.

2 **Read Phedra's diary and complete the text. Use the Past Continuous or Past Simple form of the verbs in brackets.**

On Thursday, I a) ..*was walking*.. (walk) in the gardens when I b) .... (see) Ariadne and Enarus. I c) .... (not say) hello. I d) .... (go) behind a tree to watch them. They e) .... (not talk). They f) .... (sit) on the ground. Enarus g) .... (look) into my sister's eyes and she h) .... (smile) at him.

Today, my friends and I i) .... (play) near the door of the palace when something strange j) .... (happen). I k) .... (draw) a picture busily on the ground with a stick when one of the servants l) .... (come) up to me. 'Who's that?' she m) .... (ask). 'That's my sister and Enarus,' I n) .... (answer). The servant o) .... (not say) anything but she immediately p) .... (ran) into the palace.

GRAMMAR

GRAMMAR CHECK

Verb + infinitive or –ing form

Some verbs, such as *ask, decide, learn, need, tell*, and *want*, are followed by to + infinitive.

Ariadne decided to rescue Theseus from the Minotaur.

Phedra wanted to go with Ariadne.

Some verbs, such as *enjoy, finish, go, go on, love*, and *stop*, are followed by the –ing form of the verb.

Ariadne and Enarus enjoyed talking.　　　　*Theseus stopped cleaning the boat.*

We can use either the infinitive or the –ing form with *remember*. Remember + infinitive looks forward in time and remember + –ing looks back in time.

We must remember to hurry.

Dedalus remembers teaching Enarus when he was young.

3　**Complete Ariadne's diary. Use the infinitive or *–ing* form of the verb in brackets.**

> I have decided a) <u>to run</u> (run) away with Theseus. It's all very sudden but I must stop b) .... (worry) because there are a lot of things that I need c) .... (do) very quickly.
> But one thing is important. I must go on d) .... (smile) or the servants will think that something is wrong!
> We're going to escape in a boat. Luckily, I learned e) .... (sail) with my father when I was a child and I enjoy f) .... (travel) by sea.
> I must remember g) .... (find) some gold thread. Perhaps I can ask a servant h) .... (get) me some. I also want i) .... (look for) my big cloak. I remember j) .... (see) it last week in my room, but where is it now? I love k) .... (wear) it because it's always very warm when we go l) .... (sail) in my father's boat.
> After I finish m) .... (look for) the cloak, I'll go back to Dedalus. I told him n) .... (meet) me again in about an hour.